Floating and Paddling

Contents

Written by Leon Strebor

The First Boats

Tools are used to make dug-out boats.

Dug-Out Boats

For a very long time people wanted to travel on water. They wanted to catch fish, to cross lakes, and to sail on oceans.

Many thousands of years ago, a person floated down a river on a log. In time, people learned that if they dug out the middle of the log they could sit inside it, and it did not roll over in the water. People called this boat a dug-out. The dug-out was the very first boat. For thousands of years people have made and used dug-out boats.

It takes a long time to make a dug-out boat.

People soon learned that if the ends of the log were pointed, the boat moved smoothly and quickly through the water. At first, people used their hands as paddles, but later on people found that a flat-shaped piece of wood worked much better.

People in Africa and Central and South America still use dug-out boats. They use them for fishing and for taking goods from one place to another.

Dug-out log boats are heavy.

Dug-out log boats are heavy and sit very low in the water. They cannot be used where the water is rough, because if waves wash into them they sink.

In time, people added a small log to one side of the dug-out boat to stop it from rolling over in rough water. These boats are called outrigger canoes. Outrigger canoes are still used in the Pacific Islands.

These boys are using paddles.

Boats Made from Animal Skins

For thousands of years, people have used animal skins or hides to make boats. The people of Assyria, now known as Syria, made some of the first animal-skin boats.

Coracles

People in Britain used cow hides to make little, round fishing boats. They called these boats coracles. Fishermen paddled their coracles down the river. Then the fishermen walked upstream, carrying their boats on their backs.

Canoes

Native Americans made watertight canoes from buffalo hides. They used these canoes to cross rivers.

Kayaks

The Inuit of northern North America used kayaks. They sewed sealskins together and stretched them over a wooden frame. Inuit used their sealskin kayaks on the ocean. Today, the Inuit people use canvas to make their kayaks.

Boats or Rafts?

Place	Raft	Boat	Materials Used
Africa	✘	✔	Logs
Ancient Egypt	✔	✘	Reeds
Central America	✘	✔	Bark
China	✔	✘	Bamboo
Britain	✘	✔	Cow hides, logs
North America – Indians	✘	✔	Buffalo hides, wood, and bark
North America – Inuit	✘	✔	Sealskins, wood
Pacific Islands	✘	✔	Logs
South America	✘	✔	Logs, reeds
Syria	✘	✔	Animal skins

Some Boats Around the World

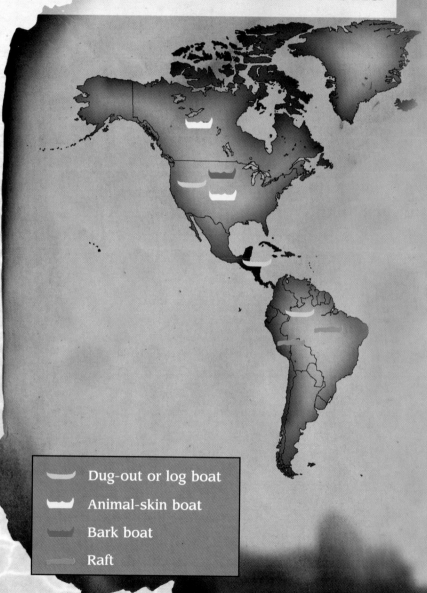

Dug-out or log boat

Animal-skin boat

Bark boat

Raft

Boats Made from Bark

The people of many countries around the world made and used canoes made of bark.

Native Americans used birch bark to make strong, light canoes that were easy to use. The Native Americans could carry these canoes past rapids and waterfalls. These canoes were very important to the Native Americans. They used them for hunting and fishing, and carrying goods from one place to another.

Bark from trees has been used by people of many countries to make canoes.

Rafts

The Ancient Egyptians made models of their rafts.

The Ancient Egyptians first made rafts from reeds. In time, they learned to tie reeds together to make long, narrow boats.

On Lake Titicaca, in South America, the same reed rafts have been made for hundreds of years. Reeds are used because trees do not grow near the lake.

People have used rafts to travel on water for almost as long as they have used dug-out boats and canoes. People make rafts by tying logs together. They also make rafts from reeds, bamboo, animal skins, or anything else that will float.

A reed raft on Lake Titicaca

Rafts from Wood and Bamboo

In Brazil, in South America, fishermen made wooden rafts with a sail. They sailed their rafts up to 30 miles (50 km) out into the Atlantic Ocean. Then they let the wind blow the rafts back to the shore again. Today, some fishermen in Brazil still use wooden rafts with sails.

In China, rafts were made using bamboo. These bamboo rafts were used to take goods to market. Some people in China still use rafts to take their goods to market today.

Rafts can be bigger and can carry more people than dug-out log boats, outrigger canoes, and kayaks. But rafts are not as safe on rough waters.

In time people wanted to be able to travel further, so bigger boats that could carry more people and goods were built.

In China, bamboo rafts are used
to take goods to market.

Glossary

A **coracle** is a small, light, round boat. A coracle is made from dried animal skins on a wooden frame.

A boat made by hollowing out the middle of a log is called a **dug-out** canoe.

Hides are another name for animal skins.

A **kayak** is an Inuit canoe made of sealskin or canvas.

An **outrigger** canoe has a long wooden frame that reaches out from the side of the canoe. This helps to balance the canoe in rough water.

Special oars with blades on the ends are called **paddles**. They are used to move a boat through the water.